Leader's Guide

Guided Meditations for
Lent, Holy Week, Easter, and Pentecost

Leader's Guide

Guided Meditations for Lent, Holy Week, Easter, and Pentecost

Jane E. Ayer

Saint Mary's Press
Christian Brothers Publications
Winona, Minnesota

Genuine recycled paper with 10% post-consumer waste.
Printed with soy-based ink.

The publishing team included Robert P. Stamschror, development editor;
Jacqueline M. Captain, copy editor; Alan S. Hanson, production editor and
typesetter; Maurine R. Twait, art director; Elaine Kohner, illustrator; cover
images © by Orion Press, International Stock Photo and © 1993 of Wayzata
Technology; pre-press, printing, and binding by the graphics division of
Saint Mary's Press.

The scriptural text throughout this book is freely adapted. These adaptations
are not to be interpreted or used as official translations of the Scriptures.

The acknowledgments continue on page 50.

Printed in the United States of America

Printing: 9 8 7 6 5 4 3

Year: 2006 05 04 03 02 01 00

ISBN 0-88489-520-3

Contents

To Shirley,

beloved friend and woman of faith,

in gratitude for the innumerable times

when shared truth became interwoven with sacred Presence

Directions ~~ *for Leading the Meditations*

LEADER PREPARATION

As the meditation leader, your preparation is especially important to the success of a guided meditation. Pray the meditation before leading a group in it. This will help you to become comfortable with its style and content. Some materials may require a brief doctrinal review with the group. By praying the meditation first, you will become aware if there is a need to do this.

If you choose to have your group do the optional art expression as follow-up to the meditations, it is best if you try it out before the group gathers to make sure it works well and to know better what directions to give.

If you intend to guide the meditations yourself rather than use the accompanying cassette or compact disc, rehearse the guided prayer, including the introductory comments, the scriptural reading, and the opening and closing prayers, so that sufficient time is allowed for the imagery to take place and for prayerful reflection to occur. The meditations should be read slowly and prayerfully, using soft instrumental music as a background.

Only a good reader who has prepared should read aloud the scriptural passage that precedes each guided meditation. The scriptural passage is important to establishing the theme and the tone of the meditation. Read it with reverence and expression, using a Bible.

PARTICIPANT PREPARATION

To introduce praying a guided meditation, it might be helpful to explain that the participants will be using a prayer form that will call upon their imagination, and that the Holy Spirit graces our imagination during prayer to help us to communicate with God. Remember that this type of prayer may not be easy for everyone in the group. Some may be self-conscious about closing their eyes; some may have difficulty getting in touch with their feelings; some may have personal obstacles in their relationship with God.

Be gentle, let go, and let the Spirit work. Sometimes it helps to reassure the participants that if they cannot "get into it" they can use the quiet time just to slow themselves down, relax, and talk to God in their own way. In fact, the participants can be told that although the meditation is guided, if the Spirit leads them in another direction, it is okay for them to go with their own reflection and not worry about the words being spoken.

A possible difficulty, one that may not be apparent at first, may be encountered by those who wear the type of contact lenses that prevent them from closing their eyes for an extended period of time. If these participants are unable to remove their lenses, invite them to put their head down, hiding their eyes in the dark crook of their arm. Another possible difficulty may be experienced by those who have a sinus problem or asthma. Instead of breathing through their nose during the deep-breathing exercises, they can breathe quietly through their mouth.

MUSIC   Quiet instrumental music is important for setting and keeping the mood of the meditation. Music can be playing even as the group gathers. It is a nice background for giving instructions. Have additional tapes or compact discs ready to play during the activities after the guided meditation. Ideally the follow-up activities will take place in a separate space; therefore, it is less disruptive if cassette or CD players are already set up in the different areas.

REFLECTION QUESTIONS   Allowing time for the participants to reflect and name the experience they have just gone through is a necessary part of these prayer experiences. The reflection questions will help the participants do this successfully. Choose several reflection questions (or use questions similar to them) and type them up, leaving room after each for a response. Make a copy for each participant. Allow enough time for each person to respond to the questions and to share his or her responses with the group. These prayer experiences are not meant to be rushed.

To avoid disrupting the quiet mood of the meditation time, pass out the reflection questions (facedown) as the participants take their places. Also give a pen or pencil to each person. If people are sitting on the floor, you could give out hardcover books or clipboards to facilitate writing. Explain that you are distributing reflection questions for use after the meditation.

Assure the participants that their responses are private and that their papers are not going to be collected. When it is time for sharing, honor and affirm all responses, and respect those persons who do not wish to answer aloud.

ART EXPRESSION AND PRAYER RITUAL (OPTIONAL)

Each prayer experience comes with an optional art expression containing a prayer ritual. You might choose to use this rather than the reflection questions, as the participants tend to share more readily with something meaningful and tangible in their hands.

If you choose to do the optional art expression, prepare the art materials ahead of time and lay them out in the area where the participants will work. Familiarize the group with the art activity before the prayer time, if possible, so as not to disrupt the meditation mood. This should allow you to give particular directions for the art activity without having to answer a lot of questions. If you have previously completed the art expression, it might be helpful to show your sample artwork at this time.

SETTING

It is imperative that the area for the prayer experience is quiet—no ringing of telephones, bells, and the like. If necessary, put a sign on the outside of your door: Praying! Please do not disturb!

Participants may sit in chairs or find a comfortable position on the floor, but they must be three or four feet from one another so that they each have their own space and do not distract one another. Therefore, the area must be large enough so the participants are not cramped. Lying down on the floor should be discouraged, as some participants are likely to fall asleep.

CENTERPIECE (OPTIONAL)

Each theme of the prayer experiences can be enhanced by creating a centerpiece that can be placed on a small table, an altar, or the middle of the floor. The centerpiece should include objects that reflect the message of the prayer, a Bible opened to the scriptural passage, and candles. For example, for the meditation on Lent ("Desert Surrender"), you might display sand, sandals, and cactus plants decoratively arranged on a brown, tan, or purple cloth.

A centerpiece for the Holy Week meditation ("Promise Keeping") might include a cross, nails, a whip (perhaps a frayed rope with knotted ends), a white garment (or a piece of cloth), a crown (or a grapevine wreath), a handmade scroll with the words from Isaiah laying open on top of the other items, and a poster with the words *promise keeping*— all displayed on a purple cloth.

To enhance the meditation on Easter ("Why Are You Crying?"), the centerpiece might consist of a makeshift tomb from a paper bag or a box positioned sideways, several stones or rocks, and a sign reading "Why are you crying?"—all positioned on a white or gold cloth.

To set the theme for the Pentecost meditation ("On Fire"), the centerpiece might display red candles, incense (if no one is allergic to it), padlocks and keys to represent the locked doors of the upper room, burning Sterno or other kinds of self-contained fires, and a white dove image—all attractively arranged on a red cloth.

MATERIALS NEEDED FOR EACH MEDITATION

- a Bible
- an audiotape or CD player
- the meditation recording or script
- tapes or CDs of instrumental music
- reflection questions (a copy for each participant)
- pens or pencils
- clipboards or hardcover books to facilitate writing, if needed
- materials for the art expression (optional; see individual project's needs)
- a centerpiece to reflect the theme (optional)
- a sign that reads Praying! Please do not disturb!

Lent
Desert Surrender

This reflective prayer experience is based on the forty days and nights that Jesus spent in self-examination as he prayed and fasted in the desert. There he was tempted by the devil, yet resisted every enticing offering because he had totally surrendered his life to the will of the Most High God. This prayer time reminds us to regard Jesus as our model of lived faith as we honestly scrutinize our life, make new choices, and value more deeply our personal ministry in building the Kingdom, which is only accomplished by totally surrendering to the Most High.

THEME   After you have given directions to the participants and set the tone for meditation, introduce the theme by saying something like the following:

Lent is the season in which we spend time in self-reflection so as to examine our life in the light of Jesus' message and mission. We need to pray deeply, as did Jesus during his sojourn in the desert; for it was during this time that his heart became fully open to receiving personal direction from the will of the Most High God. Our heart must become as open as his in order to resist temptation and surrender vulnerably and completely to the will of the Holy One. When we allow our surrender to happen, like Jesus did, we become a ready and faithful builder of the Kingdom. If we are willing to risk, entering the hush of our quiet place apart can become the desert in which to meet Jesus, our true messiah.

OPENING Read aloud this opening prayer:

Dear Jesus of desert surrender, be with us poignantly and powerfully so that our prayer time, now and always, might enlighten us to choices that come from the will of our Most High God. Allow us the grace to fully face the temptations in our life, name them, and choose against them as you did. Empower us with the realization that building the Kingdom has become our mission after your life, death, and Resurrection. Make us people of desert surrender. This is our Lenten prayer to you. Amen.

SCRIPTURE Read aloud Luke 4:1–14, using a Bible.

SCRIPT Play the "Desert Surrender" meditation on the accompanying recording, or slowly and reverently read aloud the following script for the guided meditation. Play soft, instrumental background music.

Today you will enter the hush of your quiet place and meet Jesus in your imagination. First, you will begin by doing some deep-breathing exercises.

When I say to, if you can, breathe in and out through your nose very quietly during these exercises. Close your eyes and get comfortable. You will be relaxing your entire body.

Breathe in deeply . . . hold it . . . breathe out slowly and completely. Breathe in deeply . . . hold it . . . breathe out slowly and completely. Again, breathe in deeply . . . hold it . . . breathe out slowly and completely.

Allow your feet and ankles to relax. . . . Relax your legs . . . and your hips. . . . Stay mindful of your breathing. Relax your stomach muscles . . . and now your chest. . . . Just relax. . . . Let your arms grow limp. . . . Relax your wrists, . . . your hands, . . . and your fingers. . . . Keep breathing in deeply and out slowly. Allow your shoulders to become heavy. . . . Let all the tension drain from your shoulders. . . . Relax your neck, . . . your facial muscles, . . . your forehead, . . . and even your eyelids. . . . Just relax. . . . Breathe in deeply . . . hold it . . . breathe out slowly and completely. [Pause.]

You are safely alone in the desert. . . . It is hot, and you feel the heat come from the sand beneath you and the sun above you. . . . Walk to your left and climb the sand dune that you see there. . . . As you struggle to get to the top, you notice in the distance a makeshift tent and the figure of a man sitting on a mat in front of it. . . . Continue forward, climbing down the other side of the dune toward the tent. . . . As you approach, the man sees you and rises, calling out your name in joyful greeting. . . . It is Jesus who calls to you. Hear him beckon you to come and join him. . . .

Assurance and peacefulness are in his voice as he tells you that he knows that you both have much to talk about together. . . .

You look into his face, which is brown and rugged from the sun, yet his eyes and smile are gently welcoming you and encouraging you to stay and share with him awhile. You nod your head at him as if he has spoken. . . . It will be good to retreat here in this private dwelling place with Jesus.

Jesus now offers you refreshing water to drink. . . . Accept his gift, and drink the cool water. . . . To get you out of the unaccustomed heat, Jesus thoughtfully invites you to enter his tent, which offers some protection from the sun. . . . Do not worry; it is safe to be with Jesus. . . .

Enter the tent and sit comfortably on the mat that Jesus offers to you. . . . Listen as Jesus tells you that life is full of temptations that lead away from doing God's will. . . . There is a knowing twinkle in his eye when he tells you that often the devil will sabotage you when you are praying and trying your hardest to discern and follow the will of God. . . . He reminds you that you mustn't give up or be too hard on yourself. . . . And yet, he does ask you now to share with him what three temptations are the most difficult for you to resist. . . . Take this time to be honest with yourself and Jesus. [Pause.]

Gently Jesus reaches over and places his hands around yours. . . . Hear him offer you his love, forgiveness, and understanding. . . . He tells you that he offers them to you freely to infuse within you the strength and courage that you need. . . . Hear him as he warmly promises you the grace to surrender willingly to only what God wants for you and the grace to resist any temptations that go against God's will for you. . . . Jesus is very sincere. . . . Think about what he has offered to you. With his help, can you open yourself to surrendering? . . .

Jesus tells you that his retreat in the desert has been a valuable time of being silent and listening to the Most High God speaking within him. He tells you that he also wants this kind of time for you, so that you might surrender your life to the Most High. . . . Jesus prayerfully invites you to quiet and, in the presence of the Most High God, to listen within your heart as the Most High speaks to you to help you name the ways and the means that will help you resist temptation and avoid things, situations, or people that shame you, . . . that lessen your self-love, . . . that weaken your spiritual relationship, . . . that diminish the Kingdom. . . . With the Most High God's loving guidance, spend this time soul-searching, . . . seeking out what you need from God to be faithful, like Jesus, to the living out of God's will, despite the lure of sinfulness. [Pause.]

Talk freely with Jesus now about the graces and insights the Most High has given you in your silent, reflective self-examination. [Pause.]

Jesus looks at you with tenderness. . . . Softly he tells you that he honors you for your life, . . . your pains, . . . your joys, . . . your difficult choices, . . . your new resolve, . . . and your part in the Kingdom. . . . Hear him say your name and that your God loves you. . . . As he places his two warm, strong, brown hands upon your head in blessing, he prays a prayer of surrender for you. Notice what you are feeling. . . . [Pause.]

It is time for you to leave Jesus now. Say good-bye in whatever way is comfortable for you and express to Jesus what is in your heart from having had this time with him. . . .

You leave to walk back toward the dune, and as you step halfway down its other side, you hear Jesus call out your name. Listen as his voice carries on the warm desert breeze over to you. "I am praying for you during my time of fasting. . . . You are in my heart. . . . You are in my sufferings and in my joys. . . . You are part of the Most High God's will for me. It is for you that I will someday be glorified. . . ." His last words reach you clearly in the stillness. . . . Once more, Jesus lovingly says your name and "I love you." . . . Just stand silently for a moment and let his words enfold you. . . .

Your heart is full as you follow your way back by the imprints of your earlier footsteps in the sand. . . . As you walk, allow yourself to feel the impact of your desert surrendering. . . .

Breathe in deeply . . . hold it . . . breathe out slowly and completely. Breathe in deeply . . . hold it . . . breathe out slowly and completely. Once more, breathe in deeply . . . hold it . . . breathe out slowly and completely. And when you are ready, you may open your eyes.

REFLECTION Continue to play instrumental music. Ask the participants to reflect on the experience that they have just gone through by pondering some of the following questions, or questions similar to these. You might want to suggest that they respond to the questions that speak most to them. Allow time for them to write their reflections.

• How did it feel for me to be alone in the desert?

- Was I glad to see the tent and someone there? How did I react when I saw that it was Jesus calling to me?
- Could I receive the drink of water easily from Jesus? Was I comfortable to sit and spend time with him? Why or why not?
- Have I ever experienced the devil sabotaging my efforts when I have been especially prayerful or working hard at doing God's will? If so, when?
- What were my three hardest temptations to resist that I revealed to Jesus? How did it feel to share these? Did I disclose any other areas where I needed Jesus' help?
- Did I allow myself to receive Jesus' love, forgiveness, and understanding? Did it infuse me with strength and courage?
- What were the insights that the Most High God graced me with in order to help me resist temptation? Did I freely share with Jesus how I will avoid the temptations that shame me, lessen my self-love, weaken my relationship with God, and diminish the Kingdom? What are these temptations? In what ways will I be strong enough to resist them?
- What was my emotional reaction when Jesus told me he honored me for my life, my pains, my joys, my choices, my new resolve, and my part in the Kingdom? Why did I feel that way?
- What was Jesus' prayer of surrender for me? Did his blessing move me?
- Because of my desert experience am I going to surrender more completely to God's will for me? If so, in what ways? If not, what makes it so difficult?
- In what way did I express my good-byes and my feelings toward Jesus? How did I feel about leaving him?
- Was I surprised that Jesus called to me as I was walking away? How did it make me feel to hear what he said? What struck me the most from his heartfelt words? Why?
- What is the most special message or image that I will remember from this prayer experience?

Invite and encourage the participants to share their reflections, but do not pressure them to open up. Explain that sharing faith experiences can deepen and strengthen one another's faith and that they need share only what they are comfortable disclosing to the group. Continue to play instrumental music, as it helps with reverencing the moment. Allow time for the sharing and affirming of each person.

ART EXPRESSION AND PRAYER RITUAL (OPTIONAL)

The art expression and prayer ritual is an optional activity. It can be used in place of the reflection questions. If you decide to use one of these activities, prepare the art area before the group gathers.

ART EXPRESSION 1

Set a place for each participant with newspaper to work on, various bowls of colored sand (an inexpensive alternative is mixing salt with food coloring), and a clear bottle with a lid or cork stopper. You may also substitute a piece of art paper and glue for the bottle. After the meditation, continue to play quiet music in the art area. Invite the participants to move to one of the prepared places.

Instruct the participants to fill their sand bottle or decorate their art paper using the colored sand to represent their feelings, thoughts, surrendering, or decisions evolving from their special dialog with Jesus.

ART EXPRESSION 2

Set a place for each participant with plain sand, bird gravel, or kitty litter; a sheet of heavy art paper; crayons or markers; glue; and a piece of newspaper to work on. After the meditation, continue to play quiet music in the art area. Invite the participants to move to one of the prepared places.

Instruct the participants to depict the scene in the desert by using the sand and crayons or markers. Invite them to create the desert using the sand, to draw the tent, and then to fill in the sky area or the tent with colors that express their feelings during the time spent with Jesus. Their color choices may symbolize their surrender, choices, temptations, new resolve, and so forth.

After either art project, explain that faith experiences can help strengthen one another's faith. Then invite the participants to share the effect that the prayer time had on them by asking them to explain the significance of the colors and symbolism in their artwork. Add that after they have finished describing their artwork, they are to raise it high as a sign of surrender to the will of the Most High and place it in the center of the prayer circle (or some other designated place) as a sign of the prayerful support of one another in order to surrender wholeheartedly. Perhaps they could pray, "Most High God, accept my desert surrender to your holy will in my life" or something similar as they lift up their art expression.

Allow time for the sharing and affirming of each person. Continue to play instrumental music. Remind the participants that they can return to their imagination at any time and be with Jesus in this very real way. Encourage them to place their art expression in their home in a visible spot as a reminder of their desert surrender to God's will for them.

CLOSING   For closure to the meditation experience, slowly and quietly read aloud the following prayer:

> Dear Jesus of desert surrender, we thank and praise you for the time in your tent with you; . . . for your example of prayerful retreat; . . . for your forgiveness, understanding and love; . . . for your refusal to give in to the devil's enticements; . . . for your steadfastness in following the will of the Most High; . . . for your challenge to us to name our temptations and to name what we need to resist them; . . . for your honoring of us despite our brokenness; . . . for valuing our human part in building your Kingdom; . . . for your holding of us in your sufferings and in your joys; . . . for your willingness to bring us into glory with you; . . . and for leading us into our own desert surrender in order to listen and to know the will of the Most High God in each of our lives. . . . Jesus of desert surrender, we thank and praise you. Amen.

Holy Week Promise Keeping

This empowering prayer experience, "Promise Keeping," is based on the Sabbath when Jesus stood up in the synagogue and read from the scroll of the prophet Isaiah. It was in that moment that Jesus publicly acknowledged the call of God in his life to do great acts of service that Jesus supremely fulfilled. This incident reminds us that we also need to recognize God's call in our life, ready our response, and ultimately strive to faithfully keep our promise to live out that call.

THEME   After you have given directions to the participants and set the tone for meditation, introduce the theme by saying something like the following:

> It is important for us to spend time in reflection on this reading from Holy Week so that we can hear God's call in our life, weigh what it will mean for us, make a con-

scious decision as to how we will answer it, and pledge ourselves to be faithful to it despite any suffering—just as Jesus did, right through to his torturous death on the cross. This period of reflection will also allow us to examine where we are in life areas that we have committed to in the past so that we might renew our depth of promise keeping. We can achieve this if we enter into the hush of our quiet place apart and meet Jesus, whose very life was pledged to promise keeping.

OPENING   Read aloud this opening prayer:

Jesus, you stood bravely in the synagogue and read a scriptural passage that you were meant to fulfill. Help us to see the meaning of our own life in the light of that same scriptural passage. Give us the grace to quiet our heart and mind fully so that your Spirit may empower us to hear, to act, and to be promise keepers. May the very living out of our life mirror the one that you sacrificed for us. Amen.

SCRIPTURE   Read aloud Luke 4:14–22, using a Bible.

SCRIPT   Play the "Promise Keeping" meditation on the accompanying recording, or slowly and reverently read aloud the following script for the guided meditation. Play soft, instrumental background music.

Today you will enter the hush of your quiet place and meet Jesus in your imagination. First, you will begin by doing some deep-breathing exercises. When I say to, if you can, breathe in and out through your nose very quietly during these exercises. Close your eyes and get comfortable. You will be relaxing your entire body.

　　Breathe in deeply . . . hold it . . . breathe out slowly and completely. Breathe in deeply . . . hold it . . . breathe out slowly and completely.

Again, breathe in deeply . . . hold it . . . breathe out slowly and completely.

Allow your feet and ankles to relax. . . . Relax your legs . . . and your hips. . . . Stay mindful of your breathing. Relax your stomach muscles . . . and now your chest. . . . Just relax. . . . Let your arms grow limp. . . . Relax your wrists, . . . your hands, . . . and your fingers. . . . Keep breathing in deeply and out slowly. Allow your shoulders to become heavy. . . . Let all the tension drain from your shoulders. . . . Relax your neck, . . . your facial muscles, . . . your forehead, . . . and even your eyelids. . . . Just relax. . . . Breathe in deeply . . . hold it . . . breathe out slowly and completely. [Pause.]

You are in the synagogue with a crowd of people and Jesus has just stood up to read. The scroll is given to him by the attendant. Watch as he prayerfully unrolls the scroll and finds his place. He looks around at everyone in the room before speaking, then his voice powerfully proclaims the reading from the prophet Isaiah. Listen to his words:

"The Spirit of the Lord is on me, . . .
    because he has anointed me
        to preach good news to the poor. . . .
He has sent me to proclaim freedom for the
        prisoners . . .
    and recovery of sight for the blind, . . .
        to release the oppressed,
to proclaim the year of the Lord's favor. . . ."

You watch as Jesus rolls up the scroll, returns it to the attendant, and sits down. You are aware that all eyes are on him. With quiet authority, Jesus speaks again. "Today this scripture is fulfilled in your hearing. . . ." Around you, you hear whispers.

Some people are asking each other, "Isn't this Joseph's son?"

Silently Jesus looks around the room at all the people. . . . He knows that some will not be loyal to him, . . . that some will not accept him, the carpenter's son, even as a prophet. His eyes stop and rest on you. . . . There is a mutual recognition that passes between you. Gently he weaves his way through the crowd and over to you. . . . Notice what you are feeling. . . . He greets you by name and thanks you for being here. . . . Listen as Jesus specially invites you to find a safe and quiet place with him where the two of you can talk together. . . .

You leave the synagogue and walk out to the courtyard. . . . There is a shady tree and a large rock over in the corner where both of you can sit. Jesus thoughtfully asks you if this is all right . . . and invites you to make yourself comfortable. . . .

Hear Jesus tell you that the Spirit of God is upon you. . . . Allow his words to touch you. . . . Hear him say that you are called, as he was, to fulfill the Scriptures; . . . that you are called to proclaim the Good News and liberate those who are oppressed. . . . Tenderly he tells you that you must begin with yourself first. . . . Jesus asks you to unburden the areas of your life in which you do not feel free. . . . He asks you to name the times during which you have proclaimed gossip, or something destructive, rather than the Good News. . . . He invites you to identify people whom you have imprisoned by lack of forgiveness or by being judgmental. . . . Leaning toward you and with great understanding, Jesus asks you to share with him the situations or persons whom you have not appreciated. . . . [Pause.]

He encourages you now to name fears or individuals that you allow to oppress you . . . and to talk about the things—anything—that weigh heavily upon you. . . . Take this time to continue to unveil all that is in your heart to Jesus—include past, present, or future concerns. [Pause.]

Listen as Jesus encourages you now to identify the choices you can make in order to respond to God's call to liberate yourself and others. . . . What is it that you need to do in order to celebrate the Spirit of the Lord within and around you? Tell your thoughts to Jesus and listen as he responds to what you share. [Pause.]

Warmly Jesus takes both of your hands in his and looks at you with love. . . . Jesus invites you to consider what promises you will make to fulfill what you have discussed with him. . . . Respond to Jesus with whatever promises you feel comfortable making. [Pause.]

Prayerfully Jesus anoints you on your forehead. . . . Hear what he prays just for you. [Pause.] Notice what you are feeling. . . .

It is time for Jesus to go now. Hear him say your name and thank you for all the sincerity and effort that you will be making in his name. . . . Stand and say good-bye to Jesus in whatever way is comfortable for you and that also expresses how you are feeling to have spent this time with him. . . .

Watch as he returns to the synagogue . . . toward others who need healing and liberation. . . . Sit again on the rock where you have spent these most valuable minutes with Jesus. . . . As you sit, silently reflect on what you have shared. . . . To be a true follower and imitator of Jesus, you vow that this will be your renewed time of promise keeping . . . for the Spirit of the Lord has anointed you.

Breathe in deeply . . . hold it . . . breathe out slowly and completely. Breathe in deeply . . . hold it . . . breathe out slowly and completely. Once more, breathe in deeply . . . hold it . . . breathe out slowly and completely. And when you are ready, you may open your eyes.

REFLECTION Continue to play instrumental music. Ask the participants to reflect on the experience that they have just gone through by pondering some of the following questions, or questions similar to these. You might want to suggest that they respond to the questions that speak most to them. Allow time for them to write their reflections.

- What was it like for me to be in a crowd at the synagogue listening to Jesus read the scriptural passage from Isaiah?
- What did I feel as Jesus approached me in the crowd?
- Could I allow myself to be moved when Jesus told me that the Spirit of the Lord was upon me? Why or why not?
- What areas in my life keep me from being free?
- Whom did I identify as people I might have imprisoned by being unforgiving or judgmental?
- What did I name as times that I shared gossip, or something destructive, and not the Good News?
- To what or to whom have I acted blindly?
- What fears or individuals have I allowed to oppress me?
- Was there anything else that I named to Jesus that weighs heavily upon my heart? If so, what did I name? Do I feel differently now? Why or why not?
- What choices can I make to liberate myself—and others?
- Is there something special to which I can commit to celebrate the Spirit of the Lord within me and around me as faithfully as I can?
- What did it mean to me to have Jesus thank me for all the effort I would be doing in his name?

- In what way did I express my good-bye to Jesus?
- Was it hard to see Jesus leave me? Why or why not?
- Do I believe that Holy Week can be my renewed time of promise keeping? Explain.
- What is the most special message or image that I will remember from this prayer experience?

Invite and encourage the participants to share their reflections, but do not pressure them to open up. Explain that sharing faith experiences can deepen and strengthen one another's faith and that they need share only what they are comfortable disclosing to the group. Continue to play instrumental music, as it helps with reverencing the moment. Allow time for the sharing and affirming of each person.

ART EXPRESSION AND PRAYER RITUAL (OPTIONAL)

The art expression and prayer ritual is an optional activity. It can be used in place of the reflection questions. If you decide to use one of these activities, prepare the art area before the group gathers.

ART EXPRESSION 1

Set a place for each participant with a sheet of art paper and crayons or markers. After the meditation, continue to play quiet music in the art area. Invite the participants to move to one of the prepared places.

Direct the participants to draw, in the middle of the art paper, the scene where they were sitting with Jesus on the rock under the tree. This could be done by using just abstract splashes or designs of color to depict the feelings each was experiencing from being and sharing with Jesus. Or aspiring artists may want to draw the scene in a realistic manner. Around the scene, invite the participants to use other colors to represent what their promise keeping will involve.

ART EXPRESSION 2

Set a place for each participant with a sheet of art paper and crayons or markers. After the meditation, continue to play quiet music in the art area. Invite the participants to move to one of the prepared places.

Instruct the participants to fold their paper in half lengthwise, in half widthwise, and again, widthwise. Their paper should be divided into eight sections. Now tell the group to divide each of the eight sections in half any way they choose—diagonally, horizontally, or vertically—using a crayon or marker. On one half of each of the sections, invite them to use a color to express how they were feeling about a certain issue, person, or situation before they talked to Jesus about it. On the other half of the section, have them use a color to express how they felt after sharing with Jesus. They may choose to label each section with an identifying word or words such as the following: oppression and liberation, blindness and sight, imprisoned and free, gossip and Good News, failings and promise keeping, and so on. They might not need all the sections, but suggest that one of their sections might depict their renewed pledge of promise keeping.

After either art project, explain that faith experiences can help strengthen one another's faith. Then invite the participants to share the effect the prayer time had on them by asking them to explain the significance of the colors and symbolism in their artwork. Add that after they have finished describing their artwork, they are to place it in the middle of the prayer circle (or some other designated place) and overlap the person's art expression preceding theirs. The overlapping of the artworks will be a sign that the participants will pray for one another to keep their promises to God's call in their lives. Perhaps they could say, "Jesus, help me to be as faithful a promise keeper as you were to God's call" or something similar as they lay their artwork down.

Allow time for the sharing and affirming of each person. Continue to play instrumental music. Remind the participants that they can return to their imagination at any time and be with Jesus in this very real way. Encourage them to place their art expression in their home in a visible spot to remind them of their anticipated promise keeping.

CLOSING   For closure to the meditation experience, lead the following prayer of petition:

> *Litany response*
> Jesus, help us to be faithful promise keepers.
>
> May we never forget that the Spirit of the Lord is upon us. . . . [All respond.]
>
> May each of us be guided to share the Good News rather than gossip. . . . [All respond.]
>
> May we all be graced to liberate those we have imprisoned by being unforgiving or judgmental. . . . [All respond.]
>
> May we be directed to free up the oppressed parts of ourselves and of others. . . . [All respond.]
>
> May we clearly see the situations or persons to whom we have been blind and acknowledge their presence in our life. . . . [All respond.]
>
> May each of us free ourselves from whatever weighs heavy in our heart so that we can fully celebrate the Spirit of the Lord within us and around us. . . . [All respond.]
>
> May we always humbly remember that the Spirit of the Lord has anointed us. . . . [All respond.]

Easter
Why Are You Crying?

This healing prayer experience, "Why Are You Crying?" is based on the meeting and recognition of the Risen Lord by Mary Magdalene when she met him at the site of the empty tomb. It reminds us that we also are invited to share in the mystery and miracle of the Resurrection and to truly believe that it is our story, too. It is in the midst of our tomblike experiences that our triumphant Lord offers us the power to rise above pain and receive his incredibly profound peace.

THEME   After you have given directions to the participants and set the tone for meditation, introduce the theme by saying something like the following:

> Taking time to meet and talk with the Risen Lord at the empty tomb is invaluable for each of us. Over and over again, we can be asked, "Why are you crying?" for we

have entered tombs of despair many times when our
hopes have been dashed, our faith doubtful, our life
painful, our love rejected, our losses incredible, and our
story invalidated. But we can come to experience the
peace of the Resurrection that we were meant to have, if
we silently pause now in the hush of our quiet place
apart, freely use our imagination, openly risk, and
willingly meet the Risen Jesus face-to-face.

OPENING   Read aloud this opening prayer:

Risen, glorious Lord, allow us the experience of your
felt presence as we stop in quiet prayer to spend time
with you. Grace us with the strength to face the tombs
of our life so that we can, with your help, powerfully
roll back the stones and triumphantly overcome the
shadows of our inner darkness. Give us the power to
rise victoriously and courageously above our daily
mini-deaths, as you did over your physical death. Let us
in faith hear you ask us, "Why are you crying?" so that
we might come joyfully to believe more deeply in you as
the Risen Lord and in the truth, that you—through
your life, death, and Resurrection—already hold all that
we feel pained by or see as insurmountable. Help us to
realize that with you as our Risen Lord we have no need
to cry. We ask this as your new disciples. Amen.

SCRIPTURE   Read aloud Luke 24:1–12 and John 20:10–18, using a Bible.

SCRIPT   Play the "Why Are You Crying?" meditation on the accompanying recording, or slowly and reverently read aloud the following script for the guided meditation. Play soft, instrumental background music.

Today you will enter the hush of your quiet place
and meet Jesus in your imagination. First, you
will begin by doing some deep-breathing exercises. When I say to, if you can, breathe in and out

through your nose very quietly during these exercises. Close your eyes and get comfortable. You will be relaxing your entire body.

Breathe in deeply . . . hold it . . . breathe out slowly and completely. Breathe in deeply . . . hold it . . . breathe out slowly and completely. Again, breathe in deeply . . . hold it . . . breathe out slowly and completely.

Allow your feet and ankles to relax. . . . Relax your legs . . . and your hips. . . . Stay mindful of your breathing. Relax your stomach muscles . . . and now your chest. . . . Just relax. . . . Let your arms grow limp. . . . Relax your wrists, . . . your hands, . . . and your fingers. . . . Keep breathing in deeply and out slowly.

Allow your shoulders to become heavy. . . . Let all the tension drain from your shoulders. . . . Relax your neck, . . . your facial muscles, . . . your forehead, . . . and even your eyelids. . . . Just relax. . . . Breathe in deeply . . . hold it . . . breathe out slowly and completely. [Pause.]

It is early morning, and you are walking a well-worn path with several others. You are on your way to the tomb where Jesus is buried. Mary Magdalene has invited you to come with them and to carry some of the perfumes and spices that will be needed at the burial site. The women walk with heavy hearts. Quietly they share their grief with you. . . . Their sorrow is so deep.

You hear footsteps approaching from behind. You turn and notice that a few men have caught up to your small group. They, too, are sad and share what Jesus has meant to them. . . . Their grief is evident.

In silence you walk beside Joanna, whose eyes are filled with tears. One of the women tries to comfort her, but Joanna is weeping openly now and her vision has become so blurred that she stumbles on a rock in the road, almost dropping the scented oils from her hands. You reach out to steady her. . . . In front of you, Mary Magdalene is sobbing mournfully, her head downcast, her shoulders shaking with great pain. . . . Behind you, more women and men are weeping unashamedly.

Their incredible sadness reminds you of personal situations, people, and fears that cause your heart to be troubled and tormented by despair, anger, confusion, or loss. . . . As you walk along, you allow these feelings and thoughts to surface; for here, amid your companions, you are feeling a shared kind of sorrow that unites you all.

You think quietly about events or relationships that disturb your peacefulness of heart. . . . Are these remembrances painful? . . . Are they like dark shadows casted on your living? . . . Perhaps they are not unlike the dark shadow that these women and men are experiencing due to their Lord's death.

Together your small group turns a corner in the path, and you are all facing the tomb that Joseph of Arimathea procured for Jesus' body. It is still at least fifty feet away, but it is clear that the stone has been rolled away from its entrance. The women and men begin to gasp in astonishment and some in fear. . . . Mary Magdalene breaks from the group and starts running toward the tomb shouting, "My Lord! My Lord!" . . . The rest of you begin running also. . . . Many take up her frightened chant, "Lord! Lord!" When you reach the tomb, Mary Magdalene is already coming out from within, clutching the sides of the entrance

with one hand and her stomach with the other.
. . . Her voice cracks as she informs all of you,
"His body is gone. . . ."

Along with the small crowd, you push past
her and enter the tomb. Everyone is shocked into
silence. The strips of linen that had bound his body
and the burial cloth that had been around his head
are lying neatly folded, separate from each other.
One by one, women and men start to leave the
tomb. . . . You are the last to exit. As you rejoin
the group, there is a lot of speculation as to what
has happened. Some are saying the Lord's body has
been stolen. . . . Others say that perhaps the
Apostles have taken him. . . . One is crying loudly
that it is a cruel joke. . . .

Suddenly two figures in clothes that gleam
like lightning appear. . . . Somewhat frightened,
you and your companions huddle closer together.
. . . One of the figures speaks, "Why are you
crying? . . . He is not here. He has risen on the
third day as he promised. . . . Remember? He
told you this. . . ." The figures disappear and the
decision among the group is to run and tell Peter,
John, and the others. . . .

In her sadness and bewilderment, Mary
Magdalene hesitates and does not follow the group.
. . . You decide to wait with her because she is the
one who invited you to accompany them this
morning. Alone, you are both silent, save the soft
occasional weeping from Mary Magdalene. You see
her hand go up to her cheek to brush away her
tears. You have your own tears and sorrows, but
you wish you could do something to comfort her.
Together you reverently enter the tomb where the
Lord was last lain. Mary Magdalene presses folded

hands to her chest in prayer as she stares, still weeping, at the empty space. . . .

"Why are you crying?" A white figure has filled the tomb with luminous light. You both turn, and Mary Magdalene demands through her tears, "Sir, if you have taken him, tell me where, and I will go and get him. . . ." You watch as, with gentleness, the figure reaches toward her without touching her and says, "Mary. . . ." Lovingly he looks at you and says your name, too. . . . At once, the recognition of her Lord fills Mary's heart and causes her to cry out, "Teacher! . . ." Mary Magdalene joyfully bends to hug and kiss his feet, tears of another sort cascade down her face.

Tenderly Jesus lifts her and says, "Do not hold on to me for I have need still to return to my God and your God. . . . Go and tell the others that you have seen me and that I will meet them in Galilee. . . ." There is joy in Jesus' face as he looks at his friend who quickly, gladly, and reluctantly begins to back out of the tomb to run excitedly to the others with good news. Jesus turns and express-es the same joy at seeing you there. To you, he asks, "Why are you crying? . . ."

In this moment you allow Jesus to hold all that is within your heart that pains you, causes you inner darkness, induces grievous loss, provokes paralyzing fears, and diminishes your personal power. Pour everything out to him now. His wounded palms reach out to hold it all. You have nothing to fear. [Pause.]

Again, but with humor, Jesus asks you, "Why are you crying?" . . . He is letting you know once more that he is risen, . . . that you have no reason to despair as you sometimes do, . . . that he already holds all of your anguish and lovingly transforms it by his life, death, and glorious Resurrection. . . .

Allow yourself to be more convinced and more confident than ever, as you stand before the Christ, that there is not anything that you cannot deal with—now that you have the strength and serenity of his peace enveloping you . . . transforming you.

Jesus reaches toward you and gently, briefly touches your cheek. . . . Listen as he tells you something that he wants you to remember. . . . What does he tell you? [Pause.] Is there anything that you need to say in return? [Pause.]

With loving eyes, and a voice filled with conviction, Jesus says your name and, "Peace be with you. Do not be afraid. . . ." You close your eyes for a moment to really hear and feel his words wash through you. . . . When you open them, Jesus has gone, but there is an overwhelming, comforting stillness that fills the tomb.

Revel in the peace he has given you as a gift. . . . It is true. The stone has been rolled away. There is no need to be crying now. . . .

Breathe in deeply . . . hold it . . . breathe out slowly and completely. Breathe in deeply . . . hold it . . . breathe out slowly and completely. Once more, breathe in deeply . . . hold it . . . breathe out slowly and completely. And when you are ready, you may open your eyes.

REFLECTION Continue to play instrumental music. Ask the participants to reflect on the experience that they have just gone through by pondering some of these questions, or questions similar to these. You might want to suggest that they respond to the questions that speak most to them. Allow time for them to write their reflections.

- What was I thinking and feeling as I walked with the women toward the tomb? Was I glad that Mary Magdalene had invited me? Why or why not?
- Was I surprised that men joined the group? Could I hear their grief, too?
- Whose sorrow was I most touched by? Why?
- What were my own reflections as to the pain, loss, despair, confusion, or anger that rises from some of my personal situations, relationships, fears, and dark shadows?
- What was my reaction when Mary Magdalene raced toward the open tomb?
- How did I feel as I entered the empty tomb and saw the burial cloths folded neatly?
- Did I really want to stay with Mary Magdalene, or did I want to run and tell the others? Explain.
- What were my emotions as I witnessed the reunion of Jesus and Mary Magdalene? How did I feel when Jesus spoke my name?
- What did I give Jesus to hold in our private time together? Do I feel differently now that I have been reminded that he's holding them through his life, death, and Resurrection? If so, how?
- How did it feel to have the Risen Lord gently touch my cheek? What was it that he said to me at that moment? Did I respond? If so, what did I say to him?
- Is Christ's peace pervading me? Can I believe in his words, "Do not be afraid"? Why or why not?
- Am I truly allowing myself to know that the stone is rolled back, that Jesus is risen? Do I feel his peace and realize that I have no need to cry?
- What is the most special message or image that I will remember from this prayer experience?

Invite and encourage the participants to share their reflections, but do not pressure them to open up. Explain that sharing faith experiences can deepen and strengthen one another's faith, and that they need share only what they are comfortable disclosing to the group. Continue to play instrumental music, as it helps with reverencing the moment. Allow time for the sharing and affirming of each person.

ART EXPRESSION AND PRAYER RITUAL (OPTIONAL)

The art expression and prayer ritual is an optional activity. It can be used in place of the reflection questions. If you decide to use one of these activities, prepare the art area before the group gathers.

Art Expression 1

Set each place with a 10-by-12-inch white cloth (symbolizing the burial cloth); markers, fabric pens, or puff paint; a 12-inch dowel, a 15-inch piece of yarn or ribbon; and silk flowers (optional). Have one or more glue guns available. After the meditation, continue to play quiet music in the art area. Invite the participants to move to one of the prepared places.

Direct the participants to make an Easter banner by decorating the "burial cloth" with colors, symbols, or words to describe how their prayer experience affected them. Invite them to create freely using only abstract splashes of color if they desire. Instruct them to fold over the top edge of their cloth and hot glue it so as to leave a large enough hem for the dowel to slip through. The yarn should be tied to both ends of the dowel to create a hanger. The flowers can be hot glued on the banner as well.

Art Expression 2

Set a place for each participant with newsprint, a good-sized stone or rock, poster or acrylic paints, a paintbrush, a small cup of water, and paper towels. After the meditation, continue to play quiet music in the art area. Invite the participants to move to one of the prepared places.

Direct the participants to paint an "Alleluia stone" by using colors, words, or symbols to express the things they have given to the Risen Lord to hold, their feelings after spending time with Jesus, or anything that is meaningful to them from their prayer experience.

After either art project, explain that faith experiences can help strengthen one another's faith. Then invite the participants to share the effect the prayer time had on them by asking them to explain the significance of the colors and symbolism in their artwork. Add that after they have finished describing their art expression, they are to place it in the middle of the prayer circle (or some designated place). Perhaps they could pray, "Alleluia! I have no need to cry!" or something similar as they set their artwork down.

Allow time for the sharing and affirming of each person. Continue to play instrumental music. Remind the participants that they can return to their imagination at any time and be with Jesus in this very real way. Encourage them to place their artwork in their home in a visible spot to remind them that they are an Easter people; . . . that Jesus has risen; . . . that he already holds all they are holding through his life, death, and Resurrection; . . . that he offers them a real peace; . . . and that they have no need to cry.

CLOSING For closure to the meditation experience, lead the following litany of glory:

> *Litany response*
> Alleluia! Glory! Glory to you, Risen Lord!
>
> For your Easter presence in our lives now and always
> . . . [All respond.]
>
> For your fidelity to us as you saved us without thought to your own suffering and death . . . [All respond.]
>
> For your triumphant overcoming of dark shadows, evil, and death through the great act of love of your Resurrection . . . [All respond.]
>
> For your constancy in goodness, truth, and total participation in the will of God . . . [All respond.]
>
> For your realness in your relationships to women, children, and men . . . [All respond.]

For your acceptance of all those who are marginalized and alienated . . . [All respond.]

For looking past our brokenness to see persons good and worthy of redemption . . . [All respond.]

For helping us to befriend the dark tombs of our lives and for giving us the courage to come out into the light . . . [All respond.]

For showing us the way to conquer our daily mini-deaths . . . [All respond.]

For miracles performed, then and now, in the hearts of your people . . . [All respond.]

Pentecost On Fire

This enlightening prayer experience, "On Fire," is based on the descent of the Holy Spirit upon Mary and the Apostles. It reminds us that the unique power of the Spirit is ours if we allow ourselves to be open within our mind and heart to receiving and utilizing this great gift Jesus bequested to us, his friends.

THEME   After you have given directions to the participants and set the tone for meditation, introduce the theme by saying something like the following:

> It is essential that we call on the power of the Spirit and receive this gift of the Helper that Jesus left to us, his friends. So often we try to face events, relationships, emotions, or decisions on our own, forgetting that the presence of the Spirit is freely ours. We can get in touch

with the Spirit of the Lord if we take a risk and enter
our quiet place apart.

OPENING   Read aloud this opening prayer:

> Spirit of truth and love and light, be with us in a most
> powerful way so that we might quiet and open our-
> selves to experience your touch. Help us to be confident
> that you are the same Spirit who filled the locked upper
> room, rested above and within Mary and the Apostles,
> and spoke through them in different tongues; . . .
> that you are the same Spirit who desires to burn on fire
> in our life and heart; that you are the Paraclete, the
> Helper, whom Jesus assured would be present to us al-
> ways. Grace us to meet you in the upper room in the
> hush of our quiet place apart so that we might feel your
> power and be able to rid ourselves of, or deal more se-
> curely with, life's demons that scare and immobilize us.
> We ask this in the name of your unending power. Amen.

SCRIPTURE   Read aloud Acts of the Apostles 2:1–18, using a Bible.

SCRIPT   Play the "On Fire" meditation on the accompanying recording, or slowly and reverently read aloud the following script
for the guided meditation. Play soft, instrumental background music.

> Today you will enter the hush of your quiet place
> and meet the Spirit in your imagination. First, you
> will begin by doing some deep-breathing exercises.
> When I say to, if you can, breathe in and out
> through your nose very quietly during these exer-
> cises. Close your eyes and get comfortable. You
> will be relaxing your entire body.
>   Breathe in deeply . . . hold it . . . breathe
> out slowly and completely. Breathe in deeply . . .
> hold it . . . breathe out slowly and completely.
> Again, breathe in deeply . . . hold it . . . breathe
> out slowly and completely.

Allow your feet and ankles to relax. . . .
Relax your legs . . . and your hips. . . . Stay
mindful of your breathing. Relax your stomach
muscles . . . and now your chest. . . . Just relax.
. . . Let your arms grow limp. . . . Relax your
wrists, . . . your hands, . . . and your fingers.
. . . Keep breathing in deeply and out slowly.

Allow your shoulders to become heavy. . . .
Let all the tension drain from your shoulders. . . .
Relax your neck, . . . your facial muscles, . . .
your forehead, . . . and even your eyelids. . . .
Just relax. . . . Breathe in deeply . . . hold it . . .
breathe out slowly and completely. [Pause.]

You are alone and quietly entering a building.
. . . There are stairs in front of you; . . . begin
climbing them. . . . Be careful to not make any
noise. . . . You don't want to attract any attention,
. . . for you are going to the upper room where
Mary and the Apostles are hiding from those who
would persecute them. When you get to the top of
the stairs, you walk down the hallway to a door at
the end. . . . You must knock, give your name
and a password that indicates that you are a follower of Jesus. You must do this to gain admittance.
What do you whisper into the locked door?

James, the son of Zebedee, answers and draws
you swiftly into the room. . . . You have entered
the locked room with Mary and the Apostles. The
room is full of fear and anguish. The Apostles and
their friends are being hunted to be put on trial for
being a follower of Jesus—the Jesus who has already been put to death. You understand why they
are so afraid. There is talk coming from all the
corners of the room. Thomas is doubting that they
should have ever taken up with Jesus and gotten

themselves into this mess. . . . Peter and John are trying to calm the different groups. . . .

Every once in a while John goes over to Mary to put a reassuring hand on her shoulder. Always Mary gives the same response that you see now. Calmly she looks up at John and nods into his eyes. You walk over to greet Mary, . . . and as you do, you hear Matthew wondering aloud if he believes enough, . . . if they all believe enough to be able to go through this. . . . Some of the others seem to be losing heart, too. Mary squeezes your hand and tells you to have courage and to not be afraid. . . . Gently, but firmly, she says, "My Son will not let you or anyone down. . . ."

Peter is desperately trying to keep everyone's morale up, although you sense that he, himself, is scared. . . . Mary goes to stand beside him. Listen to him as he talks with his frightened companions. . . . What does he say? [Pause.]

You stop to think about what scares you. . . . What immobilizes you so that you do not act or speak freely? . . . What fearful memories still clutch at you? . . . What demons do you wish to be rid of? . . . Who do you need to approach or what do you need to accomplish to be strong and sure of yourself? . . . What will it take for you to claim your own worth, your personality, your character, and your gifts and talents as good and valuable? . . . Find a space to sit alone in order to quietly reflect on these areas. [Pause.]

Suddenly a gust of wind fills the room. . . . People feel its surge and lose their balance. . . . Hair and veils blow in the wind. People begin to shout in fear. . . . Some who were sitting, jump up and hurry forward to huddle closely together.

. . . Some back against the wall—afraid. What do you do? What do you hear? What do you feel?

Then just as quickly as it came, the wind dies down and a hush comes over the group. . . . People begin to stand taller, straighter. . . . Some clasp hands, arms, wrists. . . . Some clasp each other's waists. . . . A fire brilliant, dancing in individual tongues, settles above each person's head. . . . You see John and Mary looking at you with joy and in wonder and awe. . . . You, too, have a flame that glows about you, yet does not burn you. . . . You can feel it. . . . You feel on fire within you. . . . The atmosphere and attitude in the room have changed drastically. . . . The air is charged with energy and fearlessness. . . . Look around you. You can hardly believe that you are in the same room with the same people. . . . Confidence, joy, courage, and astonishment fill the room. . . . Everyone starts talking simultaneously. . . .

Peter is the first to catch on to what is happening. He proclaims, loudly, "His Spirit! . . . His Spirit that he promised would be ours is here!" Some start clapping, others start hugging, still others begin singing and dancing. . . . There is no fear in this room now. Allow yourself to be part of it.

Recall now the fears and concerns you had pondered earlier. Leave the noise around you and rethink for a moment, who or what is troubling you? . . . Is your concern someone's death or dying? . . . ill health, or substance, physical, or sexual abuse? . . . an unbearable loss? . . . a critical situation at home, in your parish or community, at your job or school, or for a friend or loved one?

Regardless of the source of your anxiety, allow yourself now to look at each area with new light. . . . Feel the empowerment of the Spirit continue to spread through you with warmth. . . . With the presence of the Holy Spirit on fire within you, allow yourself new perceptions, changes in attitude, and appropriate decisions that will set you free. . . . Listen well and open yourself as a vessel to receive what the Spirit's power can give you, . . . in what the Spirit's power can direct you. . . . Speak and listen. . . . [Pause.]

The Spirit is with you. . . . You must be about your life now. . . . Are you ready? . . . Take time to say good-bye to those in the room you want to, . . . in whatever way is comfortable for you. Hear, also, what they wish for you as they gather around you. [Pause.]

One person approaches you specially. Who is it? What does this person say to you? What do you respond?

Walk toward the door. Hear choruses of "Good journey!" "God be with you!" and "Christ's peace accompany you!" Notice what you are feeling as you leave this group. . . . As you walk away, you notice that the door is not locked behind you. . . . Remember your dialog with the Spirit. Allow yourself to both accept and desire always the powerful effect this same Spirit will have on you, and through you, to those around you, and on the rest of your life. . . . Is not your heart burning within you?

Breathe in deeply . . . hold it . . . breathe out slowly and completely. Breathe in deeply . . . hold it . . . breathe out slowly and completely. Once more, breathe in deeply . . . hold it . . .

breathe out slowly and completely. And when you are ready, you may open your eyes.

REFLECTION   Continue to play instrumental music. Ask the participants to reflect on the experience that they have just gone through by pondering some of the following questions, or questions similar to these. You might want to suggest that they respond to the questions that speak most to them. Allow time for them to write their reflections.

- What did I think or feel as I went noiselessly into the building, up the stairs, and into the hall?
- What was the password that I secretly whispered into the locked door?
- How did I feel to be in the upper room with the frightened Apostles?
- When Mary spoke to me, what emotions or thoughts did I experience?
- What was Peter saying to try to reassure his companions?
- What were my reflections as I thought about what demons scare me? What immobilizes me from speaking or acting freely? What clutches at me in the form of past memories?
- Who do I need to approach and what do I need to accomplish to be strong and secure in who I am?
- How did I react to the force of wind that permeated the room? What did I hear?
- What were my feelings and thoughts as I noticed the tongues of fire settling on everyone's head? How did I feel when I realized that I, too, was being blessed?
- Could I feel the heat of the flames? Did I allow myself to be "on fire" with the Spirit?
- What was the most dramatic change in the room after the Spirit descended on all present?
- How did rethinking certain troubled areas of my life change them for me? Did I begin to see with a new perspective or attitude, and make the appropriate decisions to free myself from old demons? Explain.

- What do the Apostles wish for me as I prepare to leave?
- Who is the special person who approaches me? What is said between us?
- Will I value this experience of being on fire with the Spirit enough to have it affect the rest of my life? If so, how? If not, why not?
- What is the most special message or image that I will remember from this prayer experience?

Invite and encourage the participants to share their reflections, but do not pressure them to open up. Explain that sharing faith experiences can deepen and strengthen one another's faith and that they need share only what they are comfortable disclosing to the group. Continue to play instrumental music, as it helps with reverencing the moment. Allow time for the sharing and affirming of each person.

ART EXPRESSION AND PRAYER RITUAL (OPTIONAL)

The art expression and prayer ritual is an optional activity. It can be used in place of the reflection questions. If you decide to use one of these activities, prepare the art area before the group gathers.

Art Expression 1

Set a place for each participant with art paper, one red and one yellow piece of construction paper, markers or pens, scissors, and glue. After the meditation, continue to play quiet music in the art area. Invite the participants to move to one of the prepared places.

Direct the participants to cut flames of fire from the red and yellow construction paper and glue them on to the art paper. Invite them to label each flame with an awareness that they are taking with them from the prayer experience.

Art Expression 2

Set a place for each participant with markers or crayons, and a sheet of art paper cut in the form of a tongue of fire. After the meditation, continue to play quiet music in the art area. Invite the participants to move to one of the prepared places.

Instruct the participants to use colors, designs, words, or symbols to express the insights and feelings that they experienced in the upper room. Have them creatively and freely decorate their tongue of fire to represent what they most want to remember from this prayer experience.

After either art project, explain that faith experiences can help strengthen one another's faith. Then invite the participants to share the effect that the prayer time had on them by asking them to explain the significance of the colors, words, or symbols expressed in their artwork. Add that after they have finished describing their artwork, they are to reverently pass it around as a sign of honoring the Spirit who breathes and burns as a fire in each of us. Perhaps they could pray, "Spirit, may I always be on fire with your power and presence" or something similar as they begin to pass their art expression around.

Allow time for the sharing and affirming of each person. Continue to play instrumental music. Remind the participants that they can return to their imagination at any time and be in the presence of the Holy Spirit in this very real way. Encourage them to place their art expression in their home in a visible spot as a reminder of their time spent in the upper room, and to help them remember the Spirit on fire within them.

CLOSING   For closure to the meditation experience, have different participants share in reading aloud the following prayer of petition:

> *Litany response*
> Spirit, remain on fire within us.
>
> During the times we are face-to-face with temptation . . . socially, sexually, financially . . . [All respond.]
>
> When jealous, envious, or angry emotions direct us to lash out inappropriately at someone . . . [All respond.]
>
> For situations in which we must confront someone whom we fear or dislike . . . [All respond.]

During moments when our emotions or desires want to control or immobilize us . . . [All respond.]

At times when we need to discern and make decisions regarding our own life or someone else's . . . [All respond.]

When we lose faith and stumble because we feel abandoned, unloved, or unworthy . . . [All respond.]

During times when someone needs comfort, understanding, compassion, and the right words from us . . . [All respond.]

When we seek to deepen our spiritual relationship with you . . . [All respond.]

During times when someone we trust lets us down and we feel devalued . . . [All respond.]

In moments when we feel great pain or incredible loss . . . [All respond.]

When we allow secular possessions and attitudes, or personal complaints, relationships, or worries to consume us and displace you in our life . . . [All respond.]

ACKNOWLEDGMENTS
(continued)

To Aggie, blessings for keeping me right side up during the upside-down times of recording, publication, and life pressures.

To Barry Russo, deep appreciation for his instrumental music that reaches out to touch our soul during these meditations.

To Fr. Robert Stamschror, editor, and to the publishing team at Saint Mary's Press for their diligence in producing my work. Many thanks to each and all.

In gratitude to Anthony "Barrel" Marrapese of Reel to Real Recording Studio, Cranston, Rhode Island, for the extra that he gives through completion.

And to the other Alleluia people in my life . . . especially Isabel, Eileen, Jean, Pauline, Fr. Jude, Drea, Tom, Andre, Cheryl, Alycia, Pete, Terry, Sue, my parents, family members, retreatants, and those in my prayer circle "Woman's Voice," I am eternally grateful.

Other titles in the Quiet Place Apart series available from Saint Mary's Press

Each of the titles in this series by Jane E. Ayer (formerly Arsenault) has a leader's guide and recordings of the meditation scripts. The leader's guide contains directions for preparing the meditations, the meditation scripts, and suggestions for follow-up after the meditations. The audiocassette and the compact disc contain high-quality recordings of the meditation scripts along with a background of original music.

Guided Meditations for Advent, Christmas, New Year, and Epiphany

Leader's guide: 0-88489-517-3, 7½ x 9¼, 52 pages, stitched, $9.95
Audiocassette: 0-88489-518-1, 90 minutes, $9.95
Compact disc: 0-88489-519-X, 90 minutes, $14.95

Guided Meditations for Junior High:
Good Judgments, Gifts, Obedience, Inner Blindness

Leader's guide: 0-88489-500-9, 7½ x 9¼, 48 pages, stitched, $9.95
Audiocassette: 0-88489-501-7, 90 minutes, $8.95
Compact disc: 0-88489-502-5, 90 minutes, $14.95

Guided Meditations for Adults:
Salvation, Joy, Faith, Healing

Leader's guide: 0-88489-393-6, 7½ x 9¼, 48 pages, stitched, $9.95
Audiocassette: 0-88489-394-4, 90 minutes, $8.95
Compact disc: 0-88489-424-X, 90 minutes, $14.95

Guided Meditations for Youth on Personal Themes

These guided meditations are on the themes of new life, discipleship, self-esteem, and secrets.
Leader's guide: 0-88489-347-2, 7½ x 9¼, 46 pages, stitched, $8.95
Audiocassette: 0-88489-354-5, 90 minutes, $7.95

Guided Meditations for Youth on Sacramental Life

Jane E. Arsenault and Jean R. Cedor

These guided meditations are on the four sacraments of baptism, confirmation, the Eucharist, and reconciliation.
Leader's guide: 0-88489-308-1, 7½ x 9¼, 40 pages, stitched, $8.95
Audiocassette: 0-88489-309-X, 90 minutes, $7.95

Both parents and teens feel the "wonder and awe" of the Holy Spirit during these meditations. I know that Jane Ayer, who created these meditations, has been touched by the same Spirit. **Margie Copeland,** coordinator of religious education and youth ministry, Taunton, MA

In the nonstop day of parish life, it is good to sit in the quiet. The search for peace and tranquillity comes to an end when experiencing meditations by Jane Ayer. **Fr. John Gomes,** Our Lady of Lourdes Parish, Diocese of Fall River, MA